John Hollander

Types of Shape

New, Expanded Edition

Yale University Press

New Haven & London

Poems collected in the first edition originally appeared in *Partisan Review*, *Harper's Magazine*, the *Columbia University Forum*, *Alphabet*, *Lillabulero*, *Stereo Hi-Fi Review*, and *Poetry* (in which "Graven Image," "Crise de Cœur," "Swan and Shadow," and "Bell Curve" were first published). Some of the previously uncollected emblems in this new edition have appeared in *Book World* and in *Imaged Words and Worded Images*, ed. R. Kostelanetz. "Kitty," "Lazy Susan," "A Watched Pot," "Shadow of Noon," and "Stable Ego" were published in *Poetry*. "Kitty and Bug," which originally appeared in the *New Yorker*, is reprinted from *Harp Lake* copyright © 1988 by John Hollander, by permission of Alfred A. Knopf, Inc.

Set in Linotype Walbaum type by Tseng Information Systems, Durham, North Carolina, and The Press of A. Colish, Inc., Mount Vernon, New York.
Printed in the United States of America by Hamilton Printing Company, Castleton, New York.

Library of Congress Cataloging-in-Publication Data
Hollander, John.
   Types of shape/John Hollander.—New, expanded ed.
     p. cm.
   Includes bibliographical refernces (p.).
   ISBN 0-300-04974-9 (cloth : alk. paper).— ISBN 0-300-04925-0 (paper : alk. paper)
   I. Title.
PS3515.O3485T9 1991
811'.54—dc20   90-13017

The paper in this book meets the guidelines for permanence and durability of the Committee on Production Guidelines for Book Longevity of the Council on Library Resources.

10 9 8 7 6 5 4 3 2 1

Again,

for James Merrill,

with love and

ever-deepening

admiration

Contents

Types of Shape, which was first published in
1969, was at once a caprice and a very im-
portant book for me. Having it reissued in ex-
panded form, containing ten new poems writ-
ten since, occasions some reflections on the
problematic nature of the kind of poem it con-
tains, what writing it meant at the time, and
what occasioned the residual excursions in a
mode I thought I had finished with. At the end
of these reflections, I have added some notes on
each of the images in this book.

"Pattern poems"; *technopaignia* (a game
of artifice); *carmina figurata*; shaped poems;
Guillaume Apollinaire's term *calligrammes*;
"figured poems"—these words designate a
kind of short poem whose inscribed or printed
format presents a schematic picture of some
familiar object that is itself the subject of some
kind of emblematic meditation by the text. The
schematic picture is almost inevitably a silhou-
ette composed by the horizontal lines of verse,
which must first be of appropriate length and
then appropriately indented so as to generate
the image. Only the first of these considerations
affects the "form" of the poem; for in the mat-
ter of line length, the shaping of the silhouette
must if necessary take precedence over what-
ever prosodic conventions normally govern the
length of lines. In various languages at various
times, these can be quantitative (as in Greek

or Latin), accentual, purely syllabic, the combined accentual syllabism of verse in English, or, of course, free verse. In the last instance, the printed format itself quite simply constitutes the mode of vers libre being employed.

It is even possible to "bury" a conventional and audibly discernible verse pattern in a visual shape, and the earliest pattern poem most readers of English ever encounter is just one of these. It is Alice's "idea of the tale" told by the mouse in *Alice's Adventures in Wonderland*, as she regards his tail on the ground and listens to what the creature promises will be a "long and sad" story. The rhymed anapestic dimeters and tetrameters of the tale ("Fury said to a mouse / That he met in the house, / 'Let us both go to law: *I* will prosecute *you*.—Come, I'll take no denial: / We must have the trial; / For really this morning I've nothing to do.' ") are in a sense "hidden" in the tail shape, and only recovered in the process of reading. The *tale*/*tail* pun points up the realms of ear and eye which merge in the graphic and metrical structure of the tell-tail form:

Fury said to
a mouse, That
he met in the
house, 'Let
us both go
to law: *I*
will prose-
cute *you.*—
Come, I'll
take no de-
nial: We
must have
the trial;
For really
this morn-
ing I've
nothing
to do.'
Said the
mouse to
the cur,
Such a
trial, dear
sir. With
no jury
or judge,
would
be wast-
ing our
breath.'
'I'll be
judge,
I'll be
jury,'
said
cun-
ning
old
Fury:
'I'll
try
the
whole
cause,
and
con-
demn
you to
death'.

(It will be noticed that Carroll indicates the beginning of rhymed lines by capitalization.) As a child, I was fascinated by the interplay of visual form and audible verse; I never forgot it, and the matter of hiding audible rhythmic and even rhyming structures in free and syllabic verse has been important for me in my poetry of the past fifteen years.

In general, since Hellenistic times—from which we have a small number of shaped poems (at least one ascribed to Theocritus), such as a syrinx, the wings of Eros, an ax-head, an altar—through the nineteenth century, shaped poems have usually been considered clever, fussy tricks at best. There are many sixteenth- and seventeenth-century poems of this sort: two fine ones by George Herbert ("The Altar" and "Easter-wings") are quite well known and far from trivial. Wonderful also are many of the typographically and holographically shaped poems of Apollinaire, and I should particularly single out the remarkable work of the late May Swenson, one of the finest poets of her generation, in her magnificently imaginative book *Iconographs* (1970). I have discussed the history and nature of patterned poetry in some detail elsewhere (*Vision and Resonance*, 2d ed. [New Haven, 1985], 252–268), but I should say here that for such a poem to be anything more than clever and momentarily amusing, it must, I think, do several things.

First, it should really be a significant emblem; that is, it should work as a poem even if the shape were to be destroyed by printing all the lines flush left, and the image instead represented by a silhouette or line drawing placed above it. In that case, the poem would be like any other post-Renaissance emblem verse, meditating on some familiar object or sign and, instead of reading it for some conventional moralization ("See this anchor with a dolphin entwined in it? That means '*Festina Lente*,' as the Emperor Augustus was known to say, make haste slowly," and so on), supplying a new or revisionary kind of interpretation. Incorporating the picture into the text in the shaped poem's unique way, however, also allows the poem to talk to and of itself, in modern allegorical fashion, and *thereby* talk even more about its "subject."

Again, if the shape were transformed (into some nonsignifying projective pattern) by aligning each line flush left, the phonological and syntactic rhythms making up the part of the poem that always lies in the ear would be unaffected. The pace of going from line to line—whether and to what degree end-stopped or enjambed, which always controls rhythm in free verse—would remain. And yet here again, the augmented rhythmic effect of the patterning also allows the rate of unfolding of the text in time to keep pace with two results of the

scanning of the silhouette. The first acknowl-
edges the representational role of any part of
its contour. The second yields the purely visual
pleasure taken in that scanning, such as the
rhythm of narrowing and widening, of aug-
mentation and diminution of sheer mass, of
agitation of the right-hand edge, and of the
changing symmetries and asymmetries of right
and left contours.

Finally, there is the matter of the purely
visual pleasure taken in the composition and,
it is hoped, retrieved in the reading of poems
like these. When I began to write them, I was
seized by the puzzling delight of graphically
formal interpretation, of how to get the "ob-
ject" into possible silhouette, of dealing with
what that shadow of typography would then
be like—not only to contemplate but to plunge
into for a verse form—and of articulating lines
in response to the boundaries of outline. Get-
ting my words to do that was an insufficient
substitute for the profound pleasure that, say, a
painting of a stenciled arabic numeral by Jasper
Johns palpably takes in asking questions of an
"8" relating to pictorial space ("Is your top hole
deeper than your bottom one? Is your lower one
perhaps a round protuberance? Does this verti-
cal arc seem to support, or hang from, its adja-
cent segment?") that the ordinary use of the
sign (to *mean* "7 + 1") would never allow. But

it was an analogous pleasure, and a poetically
important one.

I have always loved visual art as much as
poetry, but am unable to paint or draw. *Types
of Shape* was as close to a book of pictures as
I would ever produce; and yet the impulses
behind it were not pictorial in themselves,
but perhaps only released these in the execu-
tion. The first time I tried anything like this
was actually in response to a musical, not a
visual, requirement—a request from a com-
poser friend, Milton Babbitt, for a song text
having something to do with time and with pre-
cisely 144 syllables (because 12 × 12?), with
some kind of clear break in the middle. I was
not at that time (around 1961) writing in the
purely syllabic verse I later used for so long,
else I should probably have composed 12 lines
of 12 syllables, or 24 of 6, or the like. Instead,
I thought of a sonnet (14 lines of 10) and—in
another poetic sense of "thought of"—of an
hourglass. Memories of both Herbert's poems
and, particularly, the Lewis Carroll tail-tale,
with its jingle "hidden" inside the shaped form,
resurfaced. What emerged was "The Shape of
Time" (printed in my 1962 collection, *Movie-
Going*), with a conventional "Shakespearean"
sonnet encoded in the shape's fluctuating lines,
the first and last of which correspond with the

"audible" feminine-ending pentameters of the sonnet's opening and closing lines:

O Time O frightened river running ever
Out beyond our reach and aiming away from us,
Actually approaching never, what
Reproach is there for an enemy
So craven? On a hidden bank
Below the quietest tree
Deep in the forest
Even, you deal
The stabbing
Blow of
Now,
Here.
Within
The moment
That's just past
A silence lies; within
The hushed glade no beating
Of the stabbed heart. The moment dead
We turn upstream and watch the widening
Flow, splashing to murder, not to avoid.
Fled is the coward, but darkly from behind us,
A frightening ally rushes to remind us.

(The sonnet's rhymes are *ever, away, never, enemy; below, forest, now, past; no, dead, flow, fled; behind us, remind us*.) The poem was "shaped" by my roughly laying out the lines so as to expand and contract and by asking the designer (fortunately, in this case, the great Harry Ford) to get the typographer to set it in the prescribed shape. I planned the form to narrow down to the words "here" and "now" at the point of constriction where the sand slips through the waist of the hourglass, at the point of the present moment where the sand accumulated below constitutes the past, and the sand remaining above, the near future. What interests me about the writing of this poem is that I now realize that as I led the sand of my words through the narrowing, I was also having them meditate on that very process.

Another minor bit of verse published in the same volume had been a handwritten document accompanying a bottle of very good burgundy (a Nuits St. Georges, if I remember right) that I had given a friend (Harold Bloom) on his thirtieth birthday. It is closer to the poems in *Types of Shape* in that the long-sloping form of the burgundy (rather than the high-shouldered shape of the claret) bottle was made by counting characters, with no punctuation. The neck of the bottle is seven ems in width, the bottom twenty-seven ems, with appropriate gradations on the way down. In the book, it was set in monotype Bembo with its variable spacing, and typographically adjusted.

                    Drop by
                    Drop it
                    Empties
                    Now not
                    Even as
                    Our own
                    Tearful
                    Vintage
                   Gathering
                   Itself with
                 Such slowness
               Gradually might
             Widen in the bottom
             Of some oblate vessel
            But as when the pouring
          Bottle now nearly half of
         Its old wine spent delivers
        The rest up in sobs rapidly
        Tears years and wine expire
        As tosspot Time sends after
        His cellarer once more alas
        Then let the darkling drops
        Wept in a decent year along
        The golden slopes elude for
        A moment or so his horribly
        Steady pouring hand and run
        Into sparkling glasses still
        Unshattered yes and undimmed

The bottle shape (like that of the flask-shaped poem in Book 5 of Rabelais's *Pantagruel*) is trivial, but the connections discovered that link aging past thirty (when years pour by more quickly), rates of pouring from actual filled and half-filled bottles, and ultimately the pace at which the poem's syntax extends along printed lines of verse anticipate the emblematic levels of my later figured poems.

   The first of these poems was another occasional verse, a presentation necessitated by debt and distance. I was living in London in the spring of 1963; shortly before I had left the United States, Ralph Kirkpatrick, the important musician, scholar of art and music, and remarkably knowledgeable lover of literature, had given me a copy of his edition of seventy Scarlatti sonatas. I had been unable then to reciprocate with anything, but I resolved to send him *something* from London. Remembering both the hourglass and the wine bottle, I decided to send him a poem in the shape of a harpsichord, viewed from above. I drew the shape in outline and then filled it in with x's on a typewriter; it occurred to me that the rectangular bench top might comprise a sort of additional or caudal stanza. Writing the text involved listing the number of x's in each line of the poem and using that list (in this case, line 1 = 1, line 2 = 2, line 3 = 5, line 4 = 8, and so on) as a "verse form." In every instance, as will be seen (the poem in question, "Playing an Obsolete Instrument," is poem number 4 of this volume), the lines are all aligned flush left—no indentation pattern is needed to articulate the shape. Rhymed lines in it to the effect that "Time untuning / everything of tightness made / attentions slip while it was played" worked their way in almost from the beginning. When it came to writing the part for the bench at the end, I remembered a favorite passage from Goethe's *Römische Elegien*, about lying in bed and tapping out hexameters on his girlfriend's bottom, that Kirkpatrick also admired; and caught up as I was in the painful matter of counting out not syllables but typed characters, the passage surfaced even more audibly. I finally resolved to put the allusive "rump" right where an actual one would be, in the middle of the bench.

The poem was duly dispatched and acknowledged, but the feel of the actual writing of it lingered, and I resolved to make another shape. I tried next an object I had acquired some months before, an Etruscan cup whose shape I loved. "A Possible Fake" (poem 2 in this volume) touched on my cycle of trivial concerns about the object itself. It had been bought at a Roman flea market, and seemed too cheap to be real (it turned out to be perfectly genuine). But my doubts about its authenticity gave way to doubts about my *own* authenticity—who should care what it is as long as it's beautiful? and so forth. In writing a poem in the shape of this cup, I kept to my earlier procedure: I would draw an outline, fill it in with x's, and contemplate the silhouette (in later instances, this sometimes took months) until I began to realize what the poem *about, in, occupying, conjured up by* its shape would also be about. In this case, I thought of the cup's mended crack and when it had suffered the injury, and of the incised black bands around it (which in this poem

I uniquely decided to acknowledge, though they could not appear in silhouette, by hiding at the appropriate point on the surface—or, as it were, in the depths of the cup—a heroic couplet that would constitute what the cup might have said, and writing this all in capital letters). Finally, the lineage of the Keats pot had to be acknowledged.

When it came to the actual writing, the matter of wide versus narrow spaces, resulting in a rhythm of long versus short lines, that had come up on the hourglass and bottle shapes raised different issues here, and the poem began to interpret the cup's, and its own, changing shape (a bowl on a column, a head on a neck). That this meditation came down to implying that what this cup ultimately "meant" was the process of its being made is important, I think. The execution of this and the harpsichord poem afforded me a way of writing short, free verse poems, of about a page in length, that would be self-contained rather than internally compartmented (with stanza-like structures), somewhat like what Wordsworth referred to when he said that Miltonic sonnets were like a dewdrop. In a sense, these and all the subsequent poems retained traces—I now realize—of the sonnet hidden in "The Shape of Time."

At various times over the next five years, I wrote twenty-three more shaped poems. My rule was always to avoid undue trickiness by never allowing a "hole" in a shape that would necessitate an ambiguity about the order of reading lines—in a letter H, say: Would one read down the first column until coming to the crossbar? Or read across both columns sequentially, ignoring the all-too-prominent gap of white space that might then separate words in order, even an article from its noun? I also wanted to keep each line of type a line of free verse and to obviate the need for a reader's scanning the text at odd angles, reading up and around a curve, for example. This necessarily, and conveniently, limited the number of silhouetted forms I could use. The procedure continued the same: a drawn outline, an x'd-in dummy providing a silhouette, a process of meditation on that, a verse format consisting of the number of syllables in each line and a note about how much the line was to be indented, and how the whole sequence was to be centered. The composition itself was frequently done on graph paper, with a box allowed for each letter; punctuation was abandoned, but capital letters began new sentences. Ultimately, no typography was involved in shaping these, in that they were composed with one em per character and required no sophistications of cold-type variable spacing. The poems commanded themselves to shape up.

When a book of these had been accumulated, the title *Types of Shape* seemed almost inevitable for me, not only because of its acknowledgment of the role of the typewriter—or a typewriter font of cold type for the composition of the book itself. The plural "types" suggested also that the "shapes"—of familiar objects, of conventional signs, of particular architectural or natural configurations—were of various sorts or types, and that the poems occupied those shapes in various types of ways: sometimes the image itself spoke, as in a sort of pictorial ecphrasis; sometimes I addressed it; sometimes I addressed a reader with respect to it, and so forth.

When the book had been assembled, I was glad to be quit of my interest in and concern for the form. I had learned a good deal about the pace and rate of unfolding of the sort of inner narrative that all lyric possesses, and was grateful for what my minor obsession had taught me. But even while the book was in press, I began to fiddle with notions for a few more of them, and over the following two decades I wrote ten more, at widely spaced intervals, which are included here. One additional, strictly exemplary, shaped poem was written for my handbook of verse form called *Rhyme's Reason*, in the purely circular shape of a much-magnified microdot, discoursing only of how it is made. It can well introduce the whole collection:

```
                This is
          a macrodot-shaped
        poem by which we mean
       not merely a disc or an
      emblematic circle which a
     text so figured might claim
    meant sun moon world eternity
   or perfection No Just a blown
  up dot in lines of 7 up to 29
   letters Past the middle the
    lines of type get shorter
     and move faster but all
      adding up to too much
         fuss about making
             a point
```

Anyone interested in looking further into the kinds of shaped poem that meditate upon the significance of their own forms must read those of the late May Swenson, in *Iconographs* (New York, 1970), and, of another sort, in *New and Selected Things Taking Place* (Boston, 1979). The Greek pattern poems can be found in J. M. Edmonds, trans., *The Greek Bucolic Poets* (Loeb Edition, 1912). The bilingual edition of Apollinaire's *Caligrammes*, translated with a commentary by Anne Hyde Greet (Berkeley and Los Angeles, 1980), is excellent; there is also a lively selection and discussion of some of them in Stefan Themerson, *Apollinaire's Lyrical Ideograms* (London, 1968). My own consideration of visual format in poetry mentioned above is the chapter "The Poem in the Eye," in *Vision and Resonance*, 2d ed. (New Haven, 1985). Anthologies of various sorts of visually patterned poetry include Berjouhi Bowler, ed., *The Word as Image* (London, 1970), Richard Kostelanetz, ed., *Imaged Words and Worded Images* (New York, 1970), Luigi Ballerini, ed., *Italian Visual Poetry, 1912–1972* (New York, 1973), and the superb exhibition catalog edited by Jeremy Adler and Ulrich Ernst, *Tezt als Figur: Visuelle Poesie von der Antike bis zur Moderne* (Wolfenbüttel, 1987). Quite separate but related questions of graphic art are explored in Mary Ellen Solt, ed., *Concrete Poetry: A World View* (Bloomington, 1968), and *Between Poetry and Painting* (Exhibition catalog, Institute of Contemporary Arts, London, 1965), and of the nature and structure of inscriptions in John Sparrow's *Line upon Line* (Cambridge, 1967), and more fully in his *Visible Words* (Cambridge, 1969).

These notes are keyed to each poem by its number in the book. A bracketed date at the end of a note indicates when the poem was composed, if it was not in the original edition.

1 "With this key," Wordsworth wrote in a sonnet about sonnets, "Shakespeare unlocked his heart"; in this poem, which I wrote in 1964 (the car did *not* have extraordinary longevity) as a prelude to what I knew was slowly becoming a sequence, I started out with a tracing of the actual key. The "opening and starting" replaces invocations to various muses, and so forth.

2 This poem is discussed above. I realize now that the "Lo, what the potter twists on his flat turning wheel" must invoke the *Kúza Náma* section of Edward FitzGerald's *Rubáiyát of Omar Khayyám* (stanzas 59–66 of the First Version), an inset sequence of quatrains on the subject of speaking pots and a Creator's hand. The actual echo is probably of Israel Zangwill's translation of the Hebrew poem from medieval France "*ki hinne kachomer,*" sung on the evening of the Day of Atonement and remembered from childhood. This trope kept haunting me, and I took it up in *Powers of Thirteen* (poems 109–111) and, most recently, in a poem called "The Mad Potter."

3 Old comic strips used to represent somebody getting an inspiration by putting into the "thought balloon" a light bulb radiating short lines, and the parenthetical gloss (IDEA!). I had always loved the more extravagantly globular shape of the larger three-way light bulbs of my childhood years, and found the discrete step-ups of brightness intriguing. This is another poem about making and Creation and suddenly imagining, but the nature of the object generating the silhouette forces it to disdain all the crescendos and decrescendos of dawn and dusk.

4 Again, this is discussed above. In the middle 1950s, when Frank Hubbard and William Dowd were building harpsichords together, I had discussed with Hubbard the possibility of his making me a lute. This never came about, and while I had my own inadequate lute in mind when I started out with "it takes too long to tune," I only now realize that in some way I was also building for myself the instrument I never had. The "Olde Musickers" I had in mind were earlier harpsichordists, vastly inferior to Kirkpatrick, the dedicatee. Perhaps the "obsolete instrument" was this kind of poetry itself.

5 The bell-shape is intriguing because, in outline as a statistical graph of distribution,

its prominence is at the top (where values are high and central to the range); but for the actual bell generating that outline, the most resonant part is at the bottom, where it rings, in more than one sense, true. When conflated, the two images imply that the least ordinary is the truest, poetically at least. "Now, for the poet, he nothing affirms, and therefore never lieth" is from Sidney's defense of poetry.

6 Plutarch's essay on the EI on Apollo's temple (at which he served as a priest) at Delphi had haunted me for years. As a poet, I have to ask whether a sign means what it may mean or, finally, what it may look like. The latter wins out here, in the end. [1989]

7 Another letter, an afterthought both to the original L (poem 8) and to the broken column (poem 30): this is not a classical ruin but a neat, neoclassical pillar, visually punning on a serifed capital I (and not, as with the typewriter's lowercase letter "l," on the digit denoting what is equal to $3 - 2$). [1987]

8 This was indeed a letter written to someone I was in love with named L——. Getting the lower serif in without violating my rule about ambiguous lineation—"holes" or "forks" in the silhouette that had to be

read around—was a delightful problem. The solution, as usual, yielded something more: parsing a strike-through with a correction written in above is a normal mode of reading, and the Proustian matter of what is lost and found in recollection was very much to the point. This was written while James Merrill's novel *The (Diblos) Notebook*, with its brilliant use of legible cancellations (rather than erasures), was in press, but I don't think that I had seen it yet. The manuscript had "initial" instead of "beginning" in the last line.

9 Again, my principle ruled out a valentine heart, because of the round-shouldered gap at the top. But that form—the conventionalized shape of a mythical idea of a site and seat of amor, rather than of a physical organ—was almost inevitable, and could be managed when rotated through ninety degrees. Which meant a fallen heart, although not quite a broken one.

10 A central emblem for this book, and for my work generally. Judaic tradition was not iconic, and in its most austere modern orthodoxies, secular poetry might as well be statues of Baal. On ancient synagogues, menorahs, and tablets of the law were carved devices; the placement of the so-called star of David on buildings and its

use as a Zionist device (in blue) is recent, although less so than the Nazis' enforcement of the star as a yellow badge. In silhouette, the interlocking of the two triangles disappears, as do the triangles themselves; only fractal ghosts of them, poking out at the corners, remain to elicit, as with the final female pubic triangle, their own readings.

11 The edge of the shadow extends only to the edge of the fabric just at high noon. The trick was, obviously, to generate the narrowest possible vertical column. This one could have been dedicated to the English Prepositions.

12 In my youth I had written a longish poem about a summer storm and a sundial whose gnomon, or motto, read HORAS TEMPESTATIS QUOQUE ENUMERO ("I also count stormy hours"). This sundial is shaped like a low one in my wife's garden; its motto is solely my own. [1990]

13 The sort of childhood treat you always remember as being bigger than it is, not just because ice cream and candy makers shrink the size of their product but because the child who contemplates their scale grows so much larger into the adult rememberer. Pauillac, a commune of the Médoc, produces much great claret.

14 A revolving tray, for condiments or whatever comestibles. The "lilies of the field, which toil not, neither do they spin" are of course from Matthew. [1990]

15 "A watched pot never boils"; but a watched emblem boils over with meaning. [1989; after another lovely evening at Chez Panisse]

16 In long-overdue acknowledgment of the long tail told in *Alice's Adventures in Wonderland*. This one is of the cat, not the mouse. [1984]

17 A second go at the silhouette, improved by Natalie Charkow's better drawing. I think that the cat has just leapt up in the air, the bug caught on its claw, and both have returned to the carpet to compose a meditative moment. [1984]

18 This was purely a quid pro quo, given to Wallace Stevens's daughter in exchange for one of his—for me—resplendently Floridian early 1940s neckties. A Ghiordes knot is one of the two principle sorts used on Oriental—mostly Turkish—carpets. I wanted to make the fabric's outline look a bit wobbly, rather than geometric.

19 At college this building formed a constant prospect, but I never knew what to make of it until I had to regard its typographic

shadow for what I could consider a commissioned poem. "Madame M" is, of course, the moon.

20 Mem Hall and Sanders Theater at Harvard were better served by the completed tower than by the flattened stump that remains. It was Stephen Orgel who in 1954 invoked the Albert buildings. Verena Tarrant met her lover here in James's *Bostonians*.

21 As one might guess, the mountain's name doesn't mean "under" anything, but derives from Woden, or Odin, or Wotan. Many hills seem to house dead heroes or kings waiting to return.

22 "Wingèd words" (*epea pteroenta*) are from Homer. The point about this is that when the arrow has hit home, the point has been taken. [1973]

23 Marvin Minsky remarked in conversation thirty-five years ago that, although no culture on earth that used an arrow sign to indicate direction probably ever did so in reverse (that is, the end opposite the point pointing the way), there's no reason why there *couldn't* be one that did. My arrow declares independence of the convention. I had already written poem 24, and figured that this arrow might as well mention pointing to that as to anything.

24 A jigsaw puzzle of the forty-eight states I had as a child cut the pieces along state lines, so I always had a strong sense of the "shape" of the various states. My own New York seemed to be both broken hatchet and T-bone steak. This poem is not about New York, however, but about nature and convention (both natural boundaries like rivers and lines drawn by surveyors are equally binding as legal borders); also, I have always felt that the Algonquian descriptive terms by which so many geographic features of the American Northeast are named haunt us (who don't even know a few simple roots, like the suffix "ett," or "ut," meaning "place at") like ghosts.

25 This is more familiar in its nongeometric form, uterine-like, curled up, in paisley patterns. Each culture that employs it in decorative motifs interprets it as signifying something else.

26 In my childhood in an observant Jewish family there were no Christmas trees. But the conventionalized form of a small spruce is unavoidable as a presence at the North American winter solstice.

27 A painter friend was explaining, in the days of so-called Op-Art, how easy it was to make colors generate a throbbing interaction. The

traditional tranquillity of the square almost cried out for subversion, and I wrote these as a sketch for his small canvas, on which the text discernibly, and painfully, appears.

28 Without a treble or bass clef, the question of the pitch of the note can't be decided. But this is mostly about the challenge of the unfilled page.

29 A "shapeless" (pointlessly articulated) typographical blob was appealing both as a limiting case and as an emblem of something going wrong. The nymph in the myth was obviously some cousin of Echo or Daphne.

30 Worrying about a broken tooth at the time came into this meditation on a familiar romantic emblem.

31 A terrestrial folding telescope, whose stepped profile was so attractive, was nonetheless a terribly poor instrument for contemplating the starry heavens above us.

32 The previous year, while in England, I reviewed James Watson's *Double Helix* in *Nature*. This seemed the yarn spun by the Fates, twisting together two strands, two lives. [1969]

33 As a schoolboy, I got the calendrical signs for the moon's first and last quarters mixed up, probably by confusing them with opening and closing parentheses read left to right. This sign also suggests the letter C as an initial of some words.

34 The *shofar* call here figured as an apocalyptic Last Trump, the form of the object fading off with its dying cry, and with the world. The scriptural passage quoted is from Amos 3.6.

35 In silhouette, all visible form translates into a common mode of shade, so that the palpable white bird and its watery reflection are here made up of identical visual material. The bottom half can thus be thought of as supporting, or depending on, the top one, and the relation of object and image seen as mutually contingent. Hence the two almost identical lines about "baring" and "bearing," occurring at reciprocal points in the images. They are equidistant from the long line of the water's surface, which also marks the "now" of a present moment (like the narrowed point of an hourglass) and thereby tentatively and momentarily implies that the object is past and the image futurity. I had violated lineation principle here for the interrogative monosyllables put by the question mark–like neck to the body behind it; in the reflection, the white space

covers sentence breaks. I suppose that a pun
on *signe* and *cygne* underlies this poem; I
was more consciously thinking of the title of
Thomas Whitaker's fine book on Yeats, and
of images, and of images of images.

Woodbridge, Connecticut
July 1990

Types of Shape

1

Skeleton key

*Opening and starting key for a
1954 Dodge junked last year.*

```
                O with what key
              shall I unlock this
            heart Tight in a coffer
          of chest something awaits a
        jab a click a sharp turn yes an
        opening Out with it then Let it
        pour into forms it molds itself
        Much like an escape of dreaming
        prisoners taking shape out in a
        relenting air in bright volumes
        unimaginable even amid anterior
        blacknesses let mine run out in
          the sunny roads Let them be
            released by modulations
              of point by bend of
              line too tiny for
              planning out back
               in hopeful dark
               times or places
              How to hold on
              to a part flat
              or wide enough
                to grasp was
                not too hard
                formerly and
                  patterned
                  edges cut
                 themselves
               What midget
                forms shall
                   fall in
                   line or
                row beyond
                 this wall
                 of self A
                  key can
               open a car
               Why not me
                O let me
                  get in
```

2

A possible fake

Black, undecorated buccherò cup,
cracked and mended,
Etruscan, bought in Rome 1963
with no questions asked.

I have given up caring whether youre genuine or not
now that I know what you have been through Slowly
shortening moments of course but the harsh snap
of the speeded—up instant and the rape of the
smooth black surface like a cracked shellac
record are authentic enough While you say
I TOO WAS EARTH ONCE STILL I YIELDED UP

FORMS POSSIBLE IN ME TO TURN MERE CUP
your fault your cracked base cannot
be seen from where I look and try
to read your heart And what you
say is true enough for mortals or
for earthen gods What bears
the weight of this so
pretentious
crown Is it
mere mire
column of
common or
even rare
clay that
carries a
proud cup
so dry so
empty now
Lo what the
potter twists
on his flat
turning wheel
is his idea and
a cup or an image
a poem or body that
turns beneath my hand O
beauty is no less true than you

3
Idea

Old Mazda lamp, 50-100-150 W.

On or
off Either darkness
unlocked again or feigned
daylight perhaps graded only by
stepped intensities fifty watts apart
In any event no continuities like those
of flickering no nor even of fading Flick
Click and there it is suddenly Oh yes I see
Indeed A mind hung brilliantly upon filaments
stung by some untongued brightness opening up
also encloses and the dark unbounded room lit
by bare bulbs collapses into an unhurting box
occupied by furniture now avoidable The dot
of closure menaces the attention which in
the flutter of eyelids can only tremble
like a nervous child lying awake lest
he be aware of the moment a closing
shutter of sleep claps to But a
snapped-off dream disperses
into darkness like gold
becoming mere motes
becoming light If
the eye lies open
to such dust as
sunlight brings
it will never
burn But that
creation make
a visible big
difference in
the way minds
look a shaper
will burn
outwardly
first and
thus once
there was
light

4
Playing an obsolete instrument

Harpsichord, 1 manual,
by Hubbard and Dowd of Boston.
Drawn from memory.

For Ralph Kirkpatrick.

O
it
takes
too long
to tune and
looks far too
fragile to be
moved about a
world stocked
with disaster
too weak even
now to move a
freighted ear
Time untuning
everything of
tightness made
attentions slip
as it was played
for Olde Musickers
while Polyhymnia and
Clio fidgeted and seven
more wearied knowing girls
fussed with their hats But then
the silliness stopped When Orpheus
took up a tom-tom once visions and
order impinged on the landscape of
fragile but wiry dreams ringing in

possibilities O now even
tapping out syllables on
a rounded rump is not as
joyful or strong a music

5
Bell curve

Normal curve of distribution.

It is the
top which
seems to an
eye untorn by tears a
kind of base not from but
on which the whole sounding
body depends Up high the most
frequent the most ordinary will
bunch together there where mean
and mode unite At such a height a
tired watcher of bells might hope
for far more sound for rounder or
rarer tones O even there at the top
for bright clear fundamentals where
most normal noises are not of chiming
but of clonk and thunk But no for the
sound of ringing is only found in the
massed metal below down there where all
frequencies of bong bing and happenings
are lower There where the bronzed embrace
surrounds the heart of air the body sounder
and the deep pounding partials far more tidal
there at the widening there there the true bell
sings all ringed about with bell-shaped roundness
Whatever the pinched arch top may assert these wide
so generous depths affirm nothing and thereby never lie
Here at bell-level nearly at the lip of truth even a sigh
will resound and trembling will be a proclamation The sound
of an hour passing is that of another coming Unskewed by will
or cracked by what in fact the case may be in the surrounding
air and
all it is
ringing O
hear it
now

6

Floating signifier

Large, problematic epsilon,
a shadow of one carved
at Delphi.

In memory of Moses Hadas.

The ancient EPSILON at the Delphic oracle set
shrewd Plutarch to brooding The second of the
vowels did it stand for the Sun of Apollo the
second planet Was it the number 5 assuring us
that five and not seven of something mattered
The E in
a carved
EI there
set up a
syllable
we could
write IF
with and
also can
mean the
simplest
of verbs
THOU ART
the THOU
being Apollo in this case and the
problematic IF being most germane
to the if—then questions directed
to oracles Plutarch submitted too
that the IF could be that IF ONLY
lying at
the core
of where
everyone
is while
he prays
to a god
But I am
not even
a priest
of later
oracular
openings
who only
murmurs of remembered powers and my easy gaze
sometimes lazily sees a patch of blank ground
swallowing up the middle prong of this simple
would—be trident letting the first Eve and my
Elizabeths go unsignified for a summer moment

7
Stable ego

Columnar capital I
of a neoclassical sort.

Any serif like
this at or
across the
top of any
high plain
column can
fully make
capital of
minuscules
or bear up
under such
burdens as
that which
I carry on
about as I
weigh this
head heavy
and dulled
with being
bearer and
borne both
Self a god
can make a
propter of
a post and
out of one
an I which
will speak
thundering
of I alone
I not some
angel no I
not any seraph

8
Love letter

*Hand-set text capital, classical,
reminiscent of the
types of Didot and Bodoni,
with pronounced serifs.*

Love begins with
light Long
glances at
ladies who
even under
this stony
blue—white
ray or its
unwarm and
unalarming
shade form
the lovely
shapes are
the lances
that break
in through
the light—
filled and
resounding
valleys we
lie across
when touch
lengthened
by longing
leads us O
my love to
a darkness
we welcome
Left alone
we can lie
clasping a
gap on two
sides like
the letter
that means   —odd
half a square hundred dark places we lay in fifty—old—
remembered times of light unending your beginning O Love

9
Crise de cœur

                          Help me
                     O help me for only
                  a brief while ago I hung red
               and yet erect in the world of wide
            white reticent backgrounds against which
         I registered Correctly placed as if pointing
      out a direction downwards towards which all must
   fall I stood firm I beat out the cut time which we
always hope we have to count on More surely than as an
emblem cut into a thick-skinned tree transfixed by a dart
perhaps I shone and signified Being all crimson and heraldic
as I was and near-kin to the promiscuous scarlet pips of cards
I was unyielding and if conventional than surely constant But as
I stood in my round-shouldered pride you struck Some fell impulse
seized me as if for a moment the surface I clung to had gone blank
like that As if a glimpse of folded arm or breast or thigh curved
under itself plunging deep into its own shadow had unhung me quite
Or as if some loss as of dry leaves blown across marble corridors
was felt for an instant even while unseen I fell tripping over a
minute lapse in lifes surface I fell heavily ah indeed flipped
over and now I lie bleeding on my sheet a sick valentine who
short of breath can barely sigh BE MINE before I fail for
even the short while that will be forever Lying here I
have blackened some and paled Yet recognizable for
what I am and unable to leap I rest uneasy Fever
warms me up towards evening after failure of
nerve has made a noon too bright to bear
bringing in place of sleep a sense
of something wrong something
half-unbroken Like
a heart

10

Graven image

The shield of David,
of no great antiquity as a
liturgical symbol.

```
                          A
                         bit
                        of an
                       image a
                      hint only
                     a momentary
                    finial like a
                   barely-glimpsed
                  porpoise possibly
       thrusting a dark shining horn through the distant water These
       should plunge one into the deeps of significance where tall
       forms stand for their maker while tides throb vast beyond
       dreaming even overhead Craving the rich dark icons ever
       denied us one day I drew upon the flat wet sand above
       the menace of foamy conquerings this hexagram which
       with the broad menorahs feathered wings was all
       the symbol we were permitted But far from the
       water of summer the sea I would gaze at the
       woven equilaterals on the synagogue wall at
       the New Year their members joined arms locked
       in legs all fondly wrought and standing for and
       on the wall unshielding be it in blue or yellow O a
       flat emblem almost a blank But as a coupling of these
       identicals used so as to seem at war how much a sign of
       love Even here though the image dives down into the wider
       part to vanish into meaning Here too in my crude making the
       end the remembered part before darkness marks a point of love
                  Let there be only
                   this final sign
                    this triangle
                     of the dark
                      about thy
                       opening
                        loves
                         own
                          V
```

11

Under the beach umbrella

At mid-day.

```
                          Straight
                  overhead now as white as
                it ever gets and fiercer than we
             can imagine the sun threatens Not with a hot
          white eye but under a cupped palms dark plot to grow
        to extend the field of shadow still no wider than our spread
      of tented blue canvas Within this dark ring is no pain White beach
    burns unbearably beyond a hot line where the edge of the noons blade
                               is
                               as
                               of
                               an
                               ax
                               To
                               go
                               by
                               it
                               so
                               as
                               to
                               be
                               in
                               or
                               at
                               or
                               on
                               it
                               is
                               to
                               be
                               of
                               it
                               as
                               we
                              all
                              are
      even alas out of it within this fragile and shifting circle of shade
```

12

Shadow of noon

*Low garden sundial, whose
gnomon asserts that it
counts sunny hours only.*

```
              1
                2
                  3
                    4
                      5
                        6
        seven eight nine ten eleven and
        here we are again at the high
                        wide center a
                        moment that
                        no sound of
                        bell defers
                        I speak but
                        four solemn
                        words HORAS
                        SOLIS SOLUM
                        ENUMERO all
                        undisclosed
                        by the wise
                        reticence a
                        silhouetted
                        form has as
                        a sole mode
                        of strength
                        And just at
                        noon a dark
                        slash touches
                        the initial S
        of the third of those
        words in acknowledgment
```

13
Eskimo Pie

*(Not to speak of Popsicle,
Creamsicle, and the rest.)*

                    I shall
                never pretend
              to have forgotten
              such loves as those
            that turned the dying
            brightness at an end of
            a childs afternoon into
            preludes To an evening of
            lamplight To a night dark
            with blanketing To mornings
            of more and more There deep
            in the old ruralities of play
            the frosted block with papery
            whisps still stuck to it kissed
            me burningly as it arose out of
            dry icy stillnesses And there now
            again I taste first its hard then
            its soft Now I am into the creamy
            treasure which to have tasted is to
            have begun to lose to the heat of a
            famished sun But O if I break faith
            with you poor dreadful popsicle may
            my mouth forget warm rains a tongue
            musty Pauillac cool skin all tastes
                          I see
                          sweet
                          drops
                          slide
                          along
                          a hot
                          stick
                          It is
                          a sad
                          sorry
                          taste
                          which
                          never
                          comes
                          to an
                          end

14
Lazy susan

She toils not neither does she spin around quickly when she
                           bears
                             a
                            lot
                          and a
                          great
                         noisome
                           lot
              of hungry hands grab at
        it all as Susan snoozes in the hall

15

A watched pot

Somewhere between a sautoir and a casserole russe, somewhat short-handled, with cover.

For Paul Bertolli and Alice Waters.

                    Not
              to mark the first
           dreaming slow whisper
of steam soon to be too hot for silences to handle
          but this still lidded form
          hiding a troubled surface
          within Boiling will sound
          deep but hollow Only what
          we have made makes scents
          Not for us the mere water
          falling away to what this
          bottom can give rise to

16
Kitty
Black domestic shorthair.

```
        O        I
       am       my
      own      way
     of being in
     view and yet
     invisible at
     once Hearing
      everything
      you see I
      see all of
     whatever you
     can have heard
     even inside the
     deep silences of
     black silhouettes
     like these images
     of furry surfaces
     darkly playing cat
     and mouse with your
     doubts about whether
     other minds can ever
     be drawn from hiding
     and made to be heard
     in inferred language
     I can speak only in
       your voice Are you
       done with my shadow
        That thread of dark
         word
          can
          all
          run
          out
          now
            and
              end
               our
              tale
```

17

Kitty and bug

Gray domestic shorthair
and black beetle.

```
         I       a
       cat      who
       coated in a
       dense shadow
       which I cast
       along myself
        absorb the
        light you
        gaze at me
        with can yet
       look at a king
       and not be seen
       to be seeing any
       more than himself
       a motionless seer
       sovereign of gray
       mirrored invisibly
       in the seeing glass
       of air Whatever I am
       seeing is part of me
       As you see me now my
       vision is wrapped in
       two green hypotheses
       darkness blossoming
        in two unseen eyes
         which pretend to be
          intent on a spot of                    bug
          upon
          the
          rug
       Who
       can
        see
         how
           eye
            can
         know
```

18
Four-in-hand

*In an exchange for a
wide, old silk one.*

For Holly Stevens.

Not Gordian nor a
Ghiordes warped
onto a bright
bit of yarn
from a rug
hiding in
high pile
No this is

not somehow

the knot of

the quotidian

which with an

as yet unmashed

panache he ties

mirrored mornings

to himself with A

holding together of

all of the reins of

the real for a time

A constant feeling of

widely bright stripes

to bind him through a

general zebra barriness

that comes between word

and word with interlinear

blanks Are these his hearts

blinds Or the binds

that almost

tie

19
Domed edifice

Low Memorial Library,
named, but no longer serving as,
the Library of Columbia University.
By Charles F. McKim.
Completed 1897.

Columbia Phi Beta Kappa Poem, 1967.

```
                    Closure
                 surmounts the
                strange open ways
              that even an interior
            may inherit or a dark chamber
           achieve through partial ruin Such
         unpierced coverings hold dominion for
        ever over minded regions below as the
      sky does above our heightened eyes that strive to measure
      and contend Not like the sole fiery lord rising wide over
      azure ramparts nor Madame M queen of all the minor purple
      distances her dust penetrated her silver honor intact Not
      like the stony rule of starlight raining in apertures cut
      to admit the once-unruined gods But from this distance or
      this angle our sunlit or unlit domes govern their domains
      as a skull tells its soft protectorate I am clamped above
      you for your own good and behold there is still visionary
      room above you We have lain below we who scanning all the
      unquiet ceilings of day and night know every zenith to be
       limned on the inner surface of some one of our domes our many
      unopening skies We have strained Our parched eyes water only by our
    lowering of them into depths of darkness and touch toward our bottom doom
```

20

Vanished mansard

The top of Memorial Hall, Harvard,
completed 1874–76,
burned down September 6, 1957.

No views from here
but always visions
of it high and red
Even when it still
sprang majestic into
the winter air there
ornate and overlooking
all the green below with
an unattainable top that
leaped into so many raised
glances and crowned nearly
all our final backward gazes
And our first glimpse placed
a heroic symbol surely between
the leaves of remembrance Even
when we said The Albert Memorial
on top of the Albert Hall See it
was in knowing that as we stood in
its long shadow we were waiting at
the brink of its green moment of new
beauty phasing in on our age like an
ease of shading a tower tenders And as
Verena Tarrant confronted her Southern
challenger under its memorial woodenness
momentous Latin lifted her own momentary
air aloft So when like the travelling case
designed for a summit or climax or triumph
or surprise it burns even now backstage in a
decade-old theatre of reminiscences black flourishings
of smoke enfold again the splendid day as an abolished
clock strikes a muffled hour Ours it was And if towers
can be owned only by viewing with their eyes all they overshadow
then our dark hearts have had it all as our wide eyes have
overseen from white impatient towers claiming the skys
brightness without thrusting toward it the red of clay
New towers are for climbing This lost peak ascended us

21

A view of the Untersberg

Elev. 6,000 ft.,
SW of Salzburg, as seen
through a window
in Schloß Leopoldskron.

                            I
                          stand
                     high on what
                    was once Odins
                  mound of power Held
                breath comes slowly leaks
            out toward high distant snows O   I
     gasp   Grasped railings sang out in the harping
   of summit air before we both reached this point After all
    our downwardings so will they ever But now our view is toward the
     white abandoned heights of distant and unreached glaciers and even to fancy
       touching them is to be lost Behind us the planar prospects reveal their plantings
 of unmown hay their beliefs that rise up to this hill only in doing strange things still
with fires on fall nights that one day Karl der Grosse may rise again from his sleep here
to conquer the mountain ghosts They haunt us too not from the summit or the climb no from
the bottom and the distance away that encases this height in rectangular frames of window
There they are at night the red ambiguous beacon at the Geireck peak and the wan necklace
of lights that marks the cable-car at unhappy Berchtesgaden But here on the plain again O
here at the bottom of the day we are changed by having been on that unreal height summits
being what they are beyond Shifting attainable lying horizons are but as useful as dreams

22

The arrow's winged word

Bull's eye, and rest of straw
target, not shown.

Ha not only is
   my flight true
      but my piercing strong My point is buried but never lost Asleep not
   dead it dreams
in a straw bed

23
This way next

I
can
point
where I
so desire
even aiming
backwards and
behind my head For who can say what I intend or mean to signify Does a
mere goal matter more than a source Does the promising arc of curved bow
not stand for more of what I mean than the childishly-colored face masking
the unresisting but unbending straw But what I may mean means nothing What I
say is what I am mistaken for Doomed by the human habits erasing eyes ever
to be a cheerful idiot I indicate the future only the failed vision of a
mere next thing a clear day a startling glance a New York State-shaped
poem on a new
page O mild
abandoned
regions
where
was
I

24
A state of nature

                              Some broken
                             Iroquois adze
                            pounded southward
                            and resembled this
                           outline once But now
                          boundaries foul-lines
                          and even sea-coasts are
                          naturally involved with
                          mappers and followers of
                          borders So that we who grew
                       up here might think That steak is
              shaped too much like New York to be real And like
           the shattered flinty implement whose ghost lives
              inside our sense of what this rough chunk should
           by right of history recall the language spoken by
           its shapers now inhabits only streams and lakes and
         hills The natural names are only a chattering and mean
       only the land they label How shall we live in a forest of
                             such murmurs with
                             no ideas but in
                             forms a state
                             whose name
                             passes
                               for
                             a city

25
The figure in the carpet

Geometrical version,
as in some Serabend and Herez rugs,
of the Boteh figure best known in
the West through Paisley prints.

Those who use the
signs know them but
for what they are And
thus this flame or leaf
a fruit or yet unflowered
uterus this cupping fig and
tongue of fire at once thrust
up in measured ranks is knotted
into life and binding necessary
yarn gets snipped So So Thus if
we know this general boteh sign
as a palm of meanings stretched
out over half of Asia what then
of the primitive of one palm or
one leaf of light only who ties
what he thinks to what he makes
so gaily and unshakingly But as
our eyes must drop to interpret
the makers gaze meets his thing
with upraised face We squint at
floors and walls or admire what
lies behind glass in shops dark
glasses lifted in the shade And
when darkness erases bright
patterns shall even the
dim paradigm remain
for those who peer so after
significances When that
all goes the carpet
is obscured not
by darkness
but our
dust

26
Midwinter Tree

A
fir
rough
against
blue snow
or a spruce
darkening the
branches of
other spruces
behind it Pines
on whitened hills
above cedar juniper
and hemlock clustered
outside a lamplit
window All of these
give over hovering or
shading after they have
been cut stood draped and
in a way made light of hung
in sparks no fire burns among
Tiers of jewels that drop
from some eye of light make
pools of color below Stain of
ruby and winking mica a starred
topaz or cold sapphires scattered
among embracing fronds extend gifts
Gems given in glistening shall endure
even now the switched-on darkness later
But eyes drop Under the asterisms
there among the aftermath of lights
showing up as shadow there is much to
be given below gems and yet beyond them
Unopened pages at the closing of the year
wide fields with tracks across them We make
our moments of fire last in this snows violet
white and in finding a kind of greenness in the
turning of white pages those ever unfallen leaves
Yes
the
old
and
new
are
adjacent not when the
summer burns but only
during the long night
From the years ground
spring stems of light

27
Squares

*For a vibrating, blue-on-red painting
by Reginald Pollack.*

This one may hurt Not by
throbbing away at vision
only no nor in the glare
where wobbling knowledge
and bright uncertainties
prevail but back there O
deep behind the curtains
of sight in an innermost
final round dark theatre
the pain is caused by no
sharp-edged light but by
the pure noumenal square

No not luminosities here
warring across the wheel
where hues cry out as if
in outrage at each other
No it is the affront the
shimmering of dreams say
of possible planes gives
to steadier phenomena as
when a standing cone cut
by an unconsciousness of
shadow frightens one who
swims in towards a beach

28
Work problem

A note without even a clef.

For Leonard Bernstein.

Across the unruled steppes stretch endless whitenesses

                              If
then governing lines of driven idea and road reach out
                              as
                              in
                              an
opening up of arms too long folded toward destinations
                              in
                              us
                              we
can barely ever dream of how easy then to see how hard
                              it
                              is
                              to
violate those snowy distances those wide possibilities
                              by
                        crotchets or
                    in vaguenesses
                unkeyed Are we sounding
                a c of noon Or
                    midnight E

29
Blots

Mistakes; losses.

For Alvin Eisenman.

                How did this ever happen
                Why gradually dear just
                as everything else does
                Like rivers cutting whitely
                and unexpectedly now through
                dark forests of prose or like
                widows left high atop
                shining pages of futurity the
              unpromising blob of language may
              reassume its visionary form
                leaving its track of utterance
                across a fecund surface finally to
                lie there a text in state awaiting
                death its scholia gathering like sculpted
                urns about it and all its great beasts
                of myth straining eternally at their
                leashes
                Or else
                it may
                 not

                And so we are left with our blotches our
                 formal horrors lying about in what cannot
               even be called pools drying into dark stains
             A painters random drip is licked up by
               some omnivore of dream and redeemed
               But our poor errors shooting out sudden pseudopods into nothingness that
               remain to reproach us like the panhandle
             of some long since abolished state
           are beyond changing We cannot even claim
           that a prior form of change came once when
            some nymph say with a lost or an unreadable
                name fled the clutches of a ravishing
                 panic grasp and was led by a relenting god
                  into the dark safety of meaninglessness of
                  colors that read as shade only of shapes
                   that suggest no mind nor hand
                    behind their making
                     But alas these unsuccesses these
                     typos and botched
                     lineaments fill up
            the spaces of conjecture cutting with the needlessly
                      hard edges by which any
                   wretched but willful roadside sign says
                        EAT refusing to blend
                  like nonsense into the general the blue

30
Broken column

For William Arrowsmith.

Are
you
too
proud
to give
up what
you can
no longer
possess
Such an
embattled
final cause
as attempting
to support by
piling up stone
on baser stone a
high impediment
to windiness is
bound to be blown
down Down there an
airy will must get
serious as winds
that can no more
than whisper about an
unyielding wish still
do their bit as brick
falls to extractions as
carious rocky drums go
smash and unfilled chunks
of jagged marble mark out on
one side the direction that a
disaster may take Thrusting up
from springing green wide lawn
and clusterings of acanthus an
assertive spike of white comes
bearing no capital no unbroken
shaft The ruin of your highest
and most visionary part may be
a burden at your age not worth
maintaining Yet under the late
sunlight your cold shadow falls across
the meadow that has reassumed your shining
terraces across our own daughters tiny
and blonde playing in and out of light Why gaze at
blue perhaps then green beyond What further shores
and what ever-unbroken marble do you strain to see

31
High upward

*Through an uncelestial old
brass folding telescope.*

O yes yes There where some
kind of center is Or pivot
from which I hang by a
cord of blindness most
often slack At the end
of a black alley along
which it is strung the
moon shrinks the small
circle of blue shimmers
In a dark beyond black
the skys peak beyond black
a piercing compass leg
points down at the top
of my head to mark the
hole in the fabric
of the world which
started to unravel
so soon after that
broad azure sphere A
itself was drawn A
glance at it would
be as useless as a
careful chart So I
dont care too much
about how terribly
painful it is when
I try to look into
it by gazing right
up and when supine
I try to pore over
the misspelled
braille so far
beyond touches
of the eye-tip
All among the
high among the
imaginables or
far behind the
unpierced dark
distant spaces
between starry
ones is closer
to all the way
down than to a
midpoint
stuck in
the dark
my right
eye I am
nearer a
low zero
a bottom
than a top
always Down is
here Up is there

32
The thread of life

Double helix.

For Francis Crick.

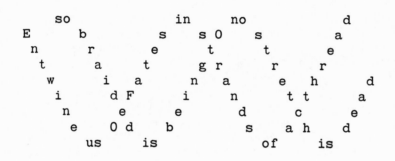

33
Last quarter

No new moon in its arms,
and yet, and yet . . .

                                                  When
                                            parentheses
                                         appear to be
                                       opening then
                                    beware of an
                                  ending Never
                                misread such
                              signs as the
                            bold crescive
                          Cs of becoming
                        or of initials
                      curving toward
                    the words like
                  Come Clear Cup
                Changes Comedy
              Crystal Create
            or even Crowns
          Their openings
        stand only for
      closings As if
    our cupped left
    hands held out
    sickle-like to
    cradle a round
    towers bulbous
    copper top cut
    some blue some
    room some hope
    out of the skys
      fierce surplus
      so these C-like
        marks close up
        But C-creatures
          grow yea truly
            behind and yet
              beyond limits
                So unrealities
                  conclude in an
                    eclipse of old
                      moonlights by
                        the darknesses
                          of origin Here
                            where the horn
                              of light thins
                                out into what
                                  is almost gone
                                    or lost a new
                                      form starts as
                                        a part of life
                                          begins

34
Tekiah Gedolah

The Last Horn-Blast, the longest
and final of the sequence of calls
blown on the shofar, *or ram's horn,*
at the New Year.

In memory of Noah Greenberg.

Who will understand its
rising intonation How
shall anyone not hear
Why will some try to
 bear to listen Shall
 a trumpet be blown in
  a city and the people
   be not afraid Or will
    the first instant last
    so long that many high
     windy cornices housing
      the self-emptying echo
       of answers unrequested
        will crumble before the
         smiling silences regain
          their rule Will her hair
           throb Will his heart itch
            Or will their eyes cloud
             up when their ears stop
              singing In a twilight
               dying winds of blast
                disperse in choirs
                 But with no west
                  where Over
                   To choke off

35
Swan and shadow

The last shape.

                    Dusk
                 Above the
             water hang the
                    loud
                    flies
                    Here
                    O so
                    gray
                    then
             What   A pale signal will appear
             When   Soon before its shadow fades
             Where   Here in this pool of opened eye
             In us   No Upon us As at the very edges
          of where we take shape in the dark air
           this object bares its image awakening
              ripples of recognition that will
                 brush darkness up into light
even after this bird this hour both drift by atop the perfect sad instant now
                 already passing out of sight
              toward yet—untroubled reflection
            this image bears its object darkening
          into memorial shades Scattered bits of
          light   No of water Or something across
          water   Breaking up No Being regathered
          soon   Yet by then a swan will have
          gone   Yes out of mind into what
            vast
            pale
            hush
            of a
           place
           past
      sudden dark as
         if a swan
            sang